Cancer Tales

in memory of
Marilyn and Grant and Rebecca

Nell Dunn

Cancer Tales

True Stories

Amber Lane Press

All rights whatsoever in any of this work are strictly reserved and application for professional or amateur performance should be made before rehearsals begin to:
Alan Brodie Representation
211 Piccadilly
London W1J 9F
E-mail: info@alanbrodie.com
No performance may be given unless a licence has been obtained.

First published in 2002 by
Amber Lane Press Ltd
Church Street
Charlbury
Oxon OX7 3PR
Telephone: 01608 810024
E-mail: info@amberlanepress.co.uk

Printed and bound in Great Britain by
Creative Print and Design Group, Harmondsworth and Ebbw Vale

ISBN: 1 872868 35 5

Foreword

Cancer Tales is in essence the voices of a number of people whose lives have been touched by cancer. True stories told in our own words.

These are private experiences that are not often shared, except with a close friend. Their value in a play is that they carry much wider truths which can touch us all. There is tremendous learning to be had here. The learning comes at a price of which we should be aware; the price includes both the actual experiences of the people involved, and the making public of issues and experiences that are intensely private.

These people whose stories are here have put on open display the ways they have coped or feel they have failed to cope with some of the huge difficulties and pain they have faced. Having this exposed in a whole domain has its own challenges; it stretches the boundaries of the private and personal, and in fact converts them into something else.

This means that you the audience have a special responsibility in the way you listen to the stories and engage with them. It is important not to become a voyeur, distanced or cocooned from what is here. Relate the stories to yourself, and your own life. Learn from them. If you can do this, then the gift that the people here are giving will be properly valued.

Joanna Howard
April 2002

Nell Dunn was born in London in 1936 and wrote her first play at her convent school when she was 11 years old: 'I remember the feeling of excitement and I wanted to be a writer. I still find writing the most interesting thing to do.'

Her first book was *Up the Junction*, which was published in 1963, and she worked with Ken Loach to turn it into a 'Wednesday Play' for the BBC. She collaborated with Ken Loach again on the film version of her second novel, *Poor Cow*, which he directed in 1967. She went on to write several more novels, including *The Incurable*, *Tear His Head Off His Shoulder*, *The Only Child* and (with Adrian Henri) *I Want*.

In 1981 Nell Dunn wrote the play *Steaming*. It was originally produced at the Theatre Royal, Stratford East and later transferred to the Comedy Theatre in the West End, where it ran for two years

Introduction

I didn't know what it meant for one person to support another through a crisis   I can remember friends and lovers going through horrific things and not knowing how to help the numb feeling of no man's land

when disaster struck in my own family I froze in a lonely world   I spoke to no one   my lips were sealed   don't come here for help, nobody at home

by writing *Cancer Tales* I got on the trail like a good detective

I begin to fathom out what it is people can do for one another

I had many long conversations with doctors and nurses and ordinary people in the front line who told me what it was like   I wrote it all down   and taking five very special women I made this play

Nell Dunn
April 2002

Acknowledgements

my greatest debt is to my friend and director Trevor Walker, who guided this work from beginning to end

my thanks to Marcia Blakenham, who said, why don't you write a play about cancer?

and my gratitude to the following people who made *Cancer Tales* happen: Clare Moynihan, who generously and repeatedly gave me both her knowledge and her experience and pointed me in the direction of so much fascinating research Professor Michael Baum, who enlightened me on what it meant to be a surgeon in breast cancer and encouraged me to go ahead Dr James Brennan, who in a noisy cafe in Bristol told me about the amazing way cancer can transform people's lives for the better Julie Friedeberger, who gave me time and whose own book on cancer, *A Visible Wound*, inspired me Dr Rob Glynne-Jones, who opened my eyes about the huge commitment cancer doctors have to their patients Dr Jane Maher for her optimism the staff of St Wilfred's Hospice, Chichester, who opened my eyes to a good death Professor Robert Souhami for telling me about the satisfaction of being a good doctor Professor Lesley Fallowfield for pointing me in fresh directions and Dr Mary Quigley, Dr Elizabeth Whipp, Dr Russell Burcombe, Dr Rosy Daniel and Patricia Pank for sharing their experience Laura Lee of 'Maggie's Centre' for her encouragement   Angela Hall, who told me about empathy

to Lloyd Trott for inviting us to RADA

and all the other kind people who had faith in me and took time from their busy lives to inform and inspire this writer– detective who knew absolutely nothing about the medical world

and for the five special women who told me their stories   my love and gratitude

Nell Dunn
April 2002

Characters

CLARE
MARY
REBECCA
JOAN
PENNY
MARILYN
SHARON
SALLY
BARBIE
GREEK DOCTOR
YOUNG DOCTOR
MR LAWRENCE
SIMON
WEST INDIAN DOCTOR
SURGEON
MAN
WOMAN

Cancer Tales was first given a rehearsed reading at the Royal Academy of Dramatic Art on 5 November 2001. It was directed by Trevor Walker with the following cast:

CLARE ... Laura Fitzpatrick

MARY ... Lavinia Bertram

REBECCA ... Katharine Gillham

JOAN ... Judy Wilson

PENNY, WOMAN ... Nancy McClean

MARILYN, SALLY, BARBIE ... Sheryl Gannaway

SHARON ... Teresa McElroy

GREEK DOCTOR, YOUNG DOCTOR, MR LAWRENCE,
SIMON, WEST INDIAN DOCTOR, SURGEON,
MAN ... Ian Redford

1. Clare

CLARE: I'm Clare   this is what happened

I was on a kind of HRT which didn't make you bleed and I was bleeding and I shouldn't be so my GP referred me to the hospital

I had a biopsy without an anaesthetic   they took a bit of the womb out   he got hold of it with some pincers and dragged it out and sliced a bit off   he was a young Greek doctor, he said

GREEK DOCTOR: if you can't take it any more you must say, and if I haven't got enough we'll bring you in as an in-patient for a night

CLARE: I want to get it over and done with   oh, and then he said

GREEK DOCTOR: thank you for being so nice to me

CLARE: it's the best thing, to hear that, thank you for being so nice to me   very sweet

GREEK DOCTOR: I know when I see a cancer and this is too clean

CLARE: he used the word clean   it evokes so much   if you have cancer you are somehow dirty

GREEK DOCTOR: we've got to cover ourselves, you must have a blood test and an ultrasound

CLARE: this took a whole month to organise and during that month I don't think about it, I am so busy   I'm a psychologist helping to care for men with testicular cancer

I went to the hospital to get the results of my tests   I'm not a bit worried   I walk in and I've got a novel with me and the doctor calls me in   it wasn't a doctor I'd ever seen before, the first doctor had entered into a relationship with me and then I never saw him again   I walk into the room with this young doctor who sat me down and said

YOUNG DOCTOR: well, we've had the results back and your ovaries are negative   we've had the ultrasound test which seems fine, nothing untoward

CLARE: and then he said

YOUNG DOCTOR: we've found a carcinoma in the uterus, actually

CLARE: and I sit there propping up my face with my hands and I said, have you?

YOUNG DOCTOR: it's very curable

CLARE: and it's as if it isn't me he's talking about and surely it's all right because everything else was negative

YOUNG DOCTOR: just a minute

CLARE: and he got up off his chair and walked out of the room and he left the door open and I am all alone and I took my notes off his desk and I read them

in the notes there was a letter from the Greek doctor who had done the biopsy   it said, this looks suspicious because she's bleeding on an HRT that she shouldn't be having any bleeding on

then when the doctor came back into the room and he sees me reading my notes and he said

YOUNG DOCTOR: those are mine

CLARE: no they're not, they're mine   and we have a little tussle

YOUNG DOCTOR: I don't know if you're meant to be reading them

CLARE: it's information about me

then he sits down again with the notes in his hand

YOUNG DOCTOR: do you realise you are going to have to have a radical hysterectomy?

CLARE: yes, I suppose that's what happens

and then I think, but I'm going away   this was the 14th of December and I was going to Africa with my sister on the 24th and I said

but I'm going on holiday to Africa in ten days

YOUNG DOCTOR: no, no, no, I don't think so   what if you feel ill when you're away?

CLARE: you've left me for a whole month   you're saying to me I may feel ill in Africa, but you've left me for a whole month walking the streets, doing my work   I might have been bleeding and I would have had no idea what was really wrong with me

and he looked at me astounded

it doesn't take a month to get a biopsy back

YOUNG DOCTOR: I don't know anything about this

CLARE: have I got to ask somebody else?

you see different people all the time and you are at somebody's mercy and you don't know who they are and they don't really introduce themselves

YOUNG DOCTOR: we're not going to be able to do this operation until the 20th of January

CLARE: but I knew who the best surgeon was and I said   I want Mr Lawrence to do this operation

then everything changed

YOUNG DOCTOR: I'd better get Mr Lawrence   he doesn't know anything about your case

CLARE: so the doctor went away for ten minutes, and then he came back with Mr Lawrence, who has a wonderful reputation for his hands

Mr Lawrence leant against the radiator and he said

MR LAWRENCE: this must have come as a terrible shock to you

CLARE: yes it has

MR LAWRENCE: at least you've got it quick

CLARE: not very quick   the hospital lost my referral letter   I had to ring you after six weeks and you said you'd never had the letter

MR LAWRENCE: these things are very slow-growing   it's a difficult thing to diagnose   we have one of the best MRI readers here and I advise you to have this done straight away

CLARE: will you do the operation?

MR LAWRENCE: I can't tell you that

CLARE: yes you can   you can   you can say yes or you can say no or you can say maybe and if you say maybe, I'm going to think again

I had friends coming to supper so I went and did the shopping   I bought lots of things for the children's stockings, thinking it doesn't matter what I spend   I was wheeling this trolley round, thinking this is reality and yet it's unreal   maybe this is all a dream

I was quite calm for a bit   when I finally let the penny drop, I felt excruciating pain

who am I to have got this? what did I do?

I tried to calm myself down   there are a myriad
of things I did or didn't do   nobody will ever
know why it happened to me

I let go of that and then I began to feel a fear that
came and went that was so frightening that I
can only begin to think of it like a young man in
a battle, in a war, alone, thinking any minute
now I am going to be sniped at   it was utter
panic but it wasn't about death   it's leaving
people   it's not just my children, it's my friends
as well

it's being left out   missing   not being there

like being young and without a mummy and a
daddy and all alone

on the other hand, there are all sorts of
things that I've done   I've had children   I've
had a marriage that went wrong   I've been
abroad   I've had a job   I've had lovers   I've
had a life   I *have* had a life   a lot of people die
much younger than that and don't have a
chance

but I'm not ready for it

2. Mary and Rebecca

MARY: my name is Mary   Rebecca is my daughter

Rebecca had been poorly for some time in Sint Maarten in the Caribbean where she was living and she came over in a mad rush to a private appointment to be seen and the doctor did a blood test and that was clear and he said there was nothing wrong with her, it was neurotic   so she went back again and got worse and her neck began to swell and the doctor in Sint Maarten told her he thought it was lymphoma and she should go back to England   he was a very nice doctor

she got in her car and drove herself round the island

she came back and we took her to our doctor and she was sent to King's and admitted the same day

the registrar who told her was extremely good   she got us in and told us too   it was leukaemia

the consultant said, you'll be here for nine months and then you'll be able to go back

she had a window to look at   it's going to be grim but she'll be coming out they did a biopsy and put in a Hickman line

the ward was good   the spirit in the ward was good   people were getting cured and Rebecca expected to get well   she was very scared and very angry   she was stroppy but very much there and dealing with it

3. Joan

JOAN: my name is Joan my daughter is Kim and my son is Grant

we were all living in Antigua my daughter Kim had been there on holiday and fallen in love with Winston, an Antiguan, and got married and stayed on well, Grant, my son, he was twenty-eight at the time and he'd lost a lot of weight, and I said to him

you haven't half lost some weight

I've been on a diet

of course he hadn't then someone said, your Grant has got a nasty cough and he said

I've been to town and got some 44 formula because I've got a little dry cough

you go into the cold air of the casino, he was working as a croupier at the time, then you come out and the heat hits you, that's what's doing it

anyway, he didn't get rid of it so I told Kim to make an appointment for him to see the doctor he goes to see the doctor and he had to have some sort of test now I didn't take anything in we were all having such good times over there what with the beach and Sonny, Kim's baby, we don't really take much notice   anyway I go and have a drink in the Spanish Main with my girlfriend, Kay, and I'm in there and all of a sudden Colin, that's Grant and Kim's father and my ex-husband and head croupier at the casino, well, in he walks   Joan, he says, Grant's got cancer   I said, what?   he said, Grant's got cancer

is he going to die?

yes, he said

well, I can't get back to Kim quick enough   I run all the way to her

what's going on?   and she said

the doctor says Grant's got cancer and they've told us to take him off the island

it only took us a few days to get home and he got an appointment at the Marsden   I took Kim's baby, Sonny, to Bishops Park and Kim went to the Marsden with Grant   when she comes to meet me at the sand pit I look up at her face and she is full of it

Mum, Grant wants to talk to you

I go to him   I got hold of his arm and we walked round the park

well, it looks like I'm going to go and see Nanny

that was my mother, who had died the year before

I can't speak properly   look Grant, we're not going to talk about it any more, we're going to fight it   and I never said another word to him about it

well, then he has to go to the hospital, and when he goes to the hospital Kim goes with him   he has to have injections every day for quite a while

then we all go back to Antigua

he has to go on with the injections out there and sometimes it was horrible   I saw him lying on the floor covered in sweat and he just couldn't take all that

we went down to the beach and lay on our backs and looked at the stars   they are so low out there it feels like you can touch them

we tried putting him on health food and we bought a machine to make carrot juice   we was there for a few weeks and then he had to come back to see the Marsden so we brought him back to London and he was beginning to look ill

and one day he can't pass any water and I panicked   I didn't know what to do and my sister-in-law rushed over and drove him to the Marsden and they put a catheter on him   he had a growth on the kidney, secondary to the lungs, but to be honest I didn't want to talk to anybody so every time Kim tried to introduce me to a doctor I said, no, that's all right

I can't face it   I don't want to

4. Penny and Marilyn

PENNY: when I first met Marilyn I had three lovers on the go   I was a very naughty girl   but later she told me

MARILYN: directly I set eyes on you I knew I was going to spend the rest of my life with you

PENNY: we went on holiday to the South of France and you discovered we were near Vence

MARILYN: we must see the Matisse chapel

PENNY: I had never been touched by Matisse

MARILYN: we went in a taxi so as not to get lost

PENNY: and here on the glass

MARILYN: through the glass

PENNY: the coloured light swept by the sunlight

MARILYN: into that small, simple space

PENNY: bathing us in blue and yellow ribbons of colour

MARILYN: there was such a sense of stillness we held our breath

PENNY: after a few minutes you turned and said

MARILYN: aren't you glad we came?

PENNY: I squeezed your hand

In the hospital she made me her next of kin

MARILYN: I want you to be treated with the same respect as a husband or wife

PENNY: the operation took seven hours and when Marilyn came round she had tubes coming out of her everywhere   as I try to make my way round the bed to get to her, it was difficult to manoeuvre so I put my hand on the drip, and it came to pieces and nearly fell apart on top of her and she said

MARILYN: oh fucking hell, Penny!

PENNY: because I'm always cack-handed, and I manage to slot it back in and in spite of her agony we are both laughing

MARILYN: then the surgeon came and she explained it was more complicated than they thought and there was a tumour the size of a melon in the womb and it had grown through the womb onto the bladder and the kidney and there were probably cancer cells in the lining of the stomach

PENNY: she said   we will know more when the results came back from the lab   and after she left, Marilyn said

MARILYN: I know it's very serious, Pen, it's you and me

PENNY: yes, we're in this together and we'll get through

I started to cry

MARILYN: Pen, it's all right to cry

PENNY: and I leant over the bed and we put our arms around each other and she faced up to it straight away

she was the strong one

MARILYN: but you're my tower of strength

PENNY: then the doctor came and told us that what Marilyn had was a carcinoma, a very rare one

MARILYN: and that it was the opposite of winning the lottery, which was rather a strange thing to say

PENNY: but that's what he said   he said he would give her a real battering with platinum chemo-therapy   she had to have six treatments   it was her only chance of survival

MARILYN: there is no choice

PENNY: I thought it would work

5. Clare

CLARE: I went on holiday and when I came back I went into hospital in the afternoon and the senior registrar came in and saw me to tell me what they were going to do and off he went   about six o'clock in the evening he came back dressed to go home with his bag slung over his shoulder and he said

I've come to ask you something and I don't like the job I've been given to do at this moment

I know you're going to ask me to go into a randomised control trial

can you imagine being asked to be in a trial the night before the operation?

and he said, we want to do a trial about the lymph nodes and whether it's better to take them out or not

what is the evidence? does the evidence say it's good to have them out?

I don't know   I'll have to come back and tell you, he said

now this was something called informed consent   he didn't know, but he was asking for my consent   he looked cross as if he expected me to just give my consent or say no way   but instead I said

well, that's very interesting, will you come back and tell me more?

anyway, he went off

it was about survival   my survival

later I was sitting there, having a cup of tea, and Mr Lawrence bustled in and closed the curtain around my bed and pointed his finger at me and said

MR LAWRENCE: no randomised trials for you   I'm taking those lymph nodes out

CLARE: he just took the whole thing out of my hands   it was brilliant

when I was just about to have the operation, Tom, the young doctor, met my son, Leo, in the corridor   I'd introduced them the night before   well, he said to Leo, Leo, he called him by his name, and he said, do you know what your mother's going to look like when she comes up from her operation?   no, said Leo   she'll look very white and wan and she'll have all these things coming out of her nose

Leo felt very included

6. Sharon

SHARON: for years I've had problems with my breasts, painful breasts, and the doctors have always said, no, you're too young to have breast cancer, forget about breast cancer, it's mastitis   then two years before I was diagnosed I had serious concerns about my left breast   I went to my lady GP and she told me exactly the same thing

it's mastitis, don't worry about it

six months later I went back again and saw a different lady doctor and she said the same thing plus

forget about it, it's your normal monthly problem

so I listened to them and for about a year whenever my breasts got swollen or painful I said to myself, no, it is mastitis, don't worry about it   well, you believe your doctor, don't you?   two different lady doctors to tell me the same thing?   you just trust them   at the time I was thirty-seven and there was no history of breast cancer in my family and it fooled them

then a year later I went back and she said exactly the same thing, she said, you're reading

too many women's magazines about breast
cancer   and then we moved

we moved here and we got a new GP   after six
months I wasn't happy about my breasts, they
were swollen again and I said to Brian, my husband, I've got to go and see this new GP and see
what he says

I phoned my mum and I said, Mum, there's a
swelling and I'm going to the doctor's and I
could hear her immediately relay it to my dad,
which I didn't want her to do, I wanted her to
hang on and to not tell him but he was sitting
there and she told him   I said, I'm going now
and I'll phone you when we get back

my husband came with me   so I went in to see
him and he took one look and he says, this is
serious

I said, get me somewhere quick, I've had this for
ages

and he sent me to the specialist two days later
and I was diagnosed with breast cancer

when we got back, Brian said

I'm going round to get your mum

they only live five minutes away   and he
brought her in and she said

you'll come through this, look what you came
through as a child

and she was trying to encourage me, but it wasn't the words   it was just for her to be present, here with me, that was the great thing   it's not that you've got to keep speaking to somebody, but for her to be with me   and it went on from there

the next week I had a mastectomy and my lymph glands removed   and I've had to put it aside that I wasn't diagnosed earlier because you can have so much anger against those doctors

7. Mary and Rebecca

MARY: I was saved by being active   Rebecca was in King's   I lived nearby   I could do things like take her washing home and get her decent food   I was working at the same time

sometimes I'd go to Sainsbury's and take in my shopping and tell her to take what she wanted and I'd take the rest home   she liked that   she'd go through it, saying

REBECCA: ugh! I don't want that   yummy, that looks good

MARY: and sometimes I couldn't do anything for her   it was her illness

she'd been away from home for years   she had lived her own life

when I was tempted to talk to the doctors or to make a fuss about something she'd say

REBECCA: get off   get out of it   let it be, Mum

MARY: I wanted to carry her away   comb her hair   do everything

when she came back from the Caribbean she had very long hair   she was going to have chemotherapy and she said

REBECCA: I've got to get my hair cut

MARY: I can cut it   I can do you a half-way cut if you like, just to get you started

REBECCA: yes, would you? I'd love that

MARY: I always used to cut their hair when they were little   so I did   cutting long hair is very hard to make it look good   it's easy for it to look just sawn off   so I thought I'll make a good job of it and try and make it like she had it before she grew it, a good shape   I knew how to cut her hair   she could trust me to make a bloody good job of it

and I did

I'm off now   I'll come back this after-noon   what would you like?

REBECCA: I'd like not to have leukaemia   have you got a cure in your bag?

MARY: her father would come in and do the crossword and fall asleep and she'd fall asleep too   I'd come in and find them both asleep

her brother James was wonderful when she was first in and had this terrible news and then she had to have this thing they screw into your pel-vis and take out some bone marrow and it's very painful whatever you do and James said

I'll go with you, Becky

they had had to have lots of injections together as children living in the tropics, so he just did it   there were times when she could just lean on him, when he was just so solid   that was part of the richness of the whole thing, being taken right down to the bones but the bones being there somehow

her sister Sara and Rebecca were very close

REBECCA: there is no one else in the world I can talk to about having hairy legs except for you, Sara   to think two months before I got sick I was thinking if only I could lose every single hair on my body

MARY: and there were Rebecca and Sara, sitting on her hospital bed, Rebecca, bald and without a single bit of hair anywhere and they both began to laugh and fall about

8. Clare

CLARE: Mr Lawrence did do the operation and he did a
         very important thing for me   I had had pre-
         meds and all the things you have   I talked to
         the anaesthetist, who was a young woman,
         please will you whisper in my ear now and then
         that I am doing very well, and she said, I will,
         even if they laugh at me

         I was in the pre-op room, and they were putting
         needles in my veins, and Mr Lawrence came out
         of the operating theatre wearing his funny little
         hat and he said

MR LAWRENCE: I want you to see, look, I'm here

         [CLARE *cries*]

CLARE: it says everything, doesn't it?

         and yet he had a brusque manner about
         him   he was very gung-ho!   very matter-of-
         fact and yet he had that sensibility

         when I came to, Leo was there, and Rosie, my
         daughter, and my sister, and I was thirsty, all
         I wanted was water   Leo gave me little wet
         sponges to suck   I wasn't allowed to drink

         then Mr Lawrence came

MR LAWRENCE: the operation went very well   I'm very
pleased

CLARE: and I could feel myself smiling an enormous
smile that spread right across my face from end
to end   that's all I wanted to hear

I was in this old-fashioned ward   the windows
were black as night   they didn't look as if they'd
been cleaned for a hundred years but the nurses
were really nice and the atmosphere was
unbelievably wonderful   I don't think I could
have been better cared for anywhere in the
world   there was a constant vigilance and
an air of real sweetness about everybody   the
doctors were there three times a day

slowly I could work out my own recovery

9. Mary and Rebecca

MARY: there was Dr Ehab, a Sudanese Moslem, and a very nice man   Rebecca was having a real hit with anger and shouting at the nurses and he went in to talk to her and when I went back in she was fine

REBECCA: he was lovely   he spoke to my fear and not to my anger and that's what I needed   he said, these are the things you might be afraid of and you don't need to be afraid of them, and he wasn't cross with me for being angry

MARY: Dr Ehab was so good at not letting her be a drama queen   he just talked to her straight all the time   she appreciated that so much, she said, about the nurses and the doctors

REBECCA: they are so good, they just help me pull myself together   they know what I'm going through

MARY: there was a very nice nurse called Sally   she would come in in the morning and say to Rebecca

SALLY: I've got a nice lot of you today   I've got you, Rebecca, and I've got Alice, all you tough guys, and this is what I like, this makes me a good day, but what you've got, Rebecca, is a really busy day   you've got x-ray, you've got blood to do, so if you're going to have a shower, have it now, because you're not going to get a minute after

MARY: she could really think through the whole day for all her patients   she was an excellent nurse

then she skipped a few days   her little boy had a meningitis scare   she came back and said

SALLY: I'm going to be a good nurse from now on

REBECCA: but you're a lovely nurse already, Sally

SALLY: I went in with my little boy   I thought he had meningitis   I had to hang around for hours at the out-patients till he was admitted   then in the ward they treated me like shit   they didn't think I knew anything, they wouldn't even let me undress him   I can see now what it's like being treated by nurses and I'm going to change

MARY: she was real as a nurse but when she had an experience of being a real patient she could see some other kind of reality was needed   she was able to learn and she was intuitive   she had her head screwed on   she thought things through   she could put it all together

10. Joan

JOAN: Grant wanted Chinese food a lot   he was eating
pretty well   we didn't have any money and the
stairs in my flat were very steep so we went to
the council and they gave us this lovely first-
floor flat and the three of us moved in with Kim's
baby, Sonny

I said we must give Grant the best we can   so
Kim borrowed some money and by this time
Grant is in a wheelchair   but he's still eating
and I'd say, well, he's going to be all right, you
can see he's eating   I won't believe he is really
ill

he was terrible with me   he never cried but he
used to hit me behind Kim's back

he just hit me, Kim! no I didn't! yes you did!
what do you keep hitting me for?

not hard, just a sly punch when I was in the
way   some days it seemed I couldn't do anything right

then he wouldn't come out of his bedroom
for three days and he wouldn't let me go in
there   he shouted at me

get out!

Kim looked after him

he grew a big beard and his hair was very curly   all I could see was a white face, even his lips were white, and his blue eyes   he looked beautiful   really beautiful   he looks like Jesus

he moved back and forth between the flat and the hospital   he was getting worse   I wouldn't talk to the doctors but they told Kim that he was likely to have a haemorrhage   so they taught Kim how to put a needle in him   they said, this was the way he's likely to go   we had to get two red towels to put in the cupboard and the needle was in the cupboard, but I didn't want to know all that

I was frightened to be left alone with him   one day Kim had to go out   she said

I won't be long

please don't leave me

she goes and Grant says

Mum, you've got to help me get in the bath

I feel awful about that because he's a big boy and I'd never seen him with no clothes on since he was little   they gave him one of these seats you put in the bath   I said, come on then, Grant, and don't worry about your dinx because I've seen that when you was a baby, so don't worry about that anyway, I help him, and I wash his back, and he has a real nice bath and he said

I really enjoyed that

we was all right   it was just me and him

and when Kim came back I said

we've actually had a bath, more or less together here

next day he wanted to go back to the hospital and he never came out no more

11. Penny and Marilyn

PENNY: after the first lot of chemo she came home and she is in a lot of pain

MARILYN: I was very poorly　very poorly indeed

PENNY: she had morphine patches and liquid morphine

MARILYN: I began to feel a little better

PENNY: I had never cooked, she had always been the cook

MARILYN: but she learnt to cook all my favourite dishes

PENNY: I became as good as Delia Smith

MARILYN: and I put on eight pounds!

PENNY: an enormous euphoria

MARILYN: we listen to the 'Emperor Concerto'

PENNY: and Barbra Streisand　we watch our French and Saunders videos

MARILYN: and *The Life of Birds*　then the second chemo　and one of the nurses put the wrong lead on the box and so instead of going through in twenty-four hours it goes through in fifteen hours there is a big notice in the ward which says: 'Nurses please make sure you put the right lead in for giving chemotherapy – the wrong lead can be very dangerous'

PENNY: she is very ill   there aren't enough nurses patients are calling out for the nurse

MARILYN: nurse!

PENNY: they are in pain   she is in pain

I ask for a room of our own and I move in and take care of her   we are there for two weeks   I do everything except give her the chemo

MARILYN: I had to have a blood transfusion   it was meant to go in in four hours   instead the bag was empty in forty minutes   the clip that allows the flow had been incorrectly adjusted   the nurse apologised

PENNY: she is in dreadful pain   the doctor said there was nothing more to be done

MARILYN: it is in my back   please, please re-examine my scan

PENNY: and later he comes in and says

I'm sorry, there is another tumour on the back of the pelvis   we didn't see it before because we weren't looking for it

but you get to a stage where it's no good being angry   Marilyn is in pain and what can I do?

MARILYN: he says, you'll have to have radiotherapy on that one, the chemo won't touch it

PENNY: as soon as she could walk with the drip she wanted to go home

MARILYN: Pen, I want to go home

PENNY: she can walk with a stick but she is losing weight rapidly   I can't tempt her to eat

MARILYN: the district nurses come   the Macmillan nurse comes   they are all wonderful

PENNY: Marilyn sits at her desk and books a cruise for us in the spring

MARILYN: it is going to be the holiday of a lifetime   if anything happens to me, Pen, take your mum

PENNY: she gets the lawyer round and she sorts out everything

MARILYN: all my affairs are in order

12. Clare

CLARE: when the whole picture came back it was found it had gone into one lymph node

I was in the waiting room   Abigail, my oncologist, came in, she was dressed in an Armani trouser suit, she is tall, very, very tall and slender   she's got black curly hair and is very alive   I went into her room and she said

we are going to throw everything at you because of this node   we are going to give external beam radiotherapy into the pelvis

she told me because the tumour was angry I was also going to have to have brachia therapy, which is when they put the radiotherapy up into your vagina   they do that to try and stop it recurring

I like Abigail

13. Sharon

SHARON: my consultant surgeon told me I would need radiotherapy and chemotherapy so he sent me to Dr Quigley at Oldchurch Hospital   when I meet her I say, I want as much treatment as possible   I want to get well

Mum and I would go to chemotherapy and from there we'd go shopping, down to Romford   she'd say

come on, we'll stay out for a little bit longer

that was her way of helping me through it   it's not so much the worry   of course I was worried, but with my mother and my friends I could talk about the worries because you don't tell everybody   but the people close to me knew how I struggled the first few months and I haven't got severe depression   that's amazing

I feel sad for people who've got nobody to turn to   it must be hard if you're on your own   now my husband, every appointment I ever have with the surgeon or with Dr Quigley, he's there   and if I haven't got a question to ask then he may have a question to ask

I've known Brian since I was fifteen and we got married when I was nineteen   and when I lost

my breast and people said to me, what about
your husband? well, I had no qualms at all I
know my husband so well, it just wouldn't
bother him he's more worried about me fight-
ing for my life than losing a breast no, it didn't
even cross my mind and for me directly, I
knew my breast was cancerous I rejected it I
wanted it gone

I've never cried over the loss of my breast

I researched breast cancer I asked Dr Quigley
to remove my ovaries and she said, we can put
you on Zoladex, it's a new treatment and it can
be reversed, your ovaries will shut down for a
certain period of time but they can recover
and it's not as bad as having your ovaries removed so I also had monthly injections of
Zoladex that stops your ovaries producing
oestrogen

that was difficult because it gave me all the
symptoms of the menopause, the hot flushes,
the lot the sweat would run off my arms and
drip down my hands because of my age my
body wasn't prepared and I lost bone density,
so now I take Dydronol to help me build bone

I wasn't born with strength I work my way
towards it, definitely even understanding the
medical language I've always had an interest

to go for tests and to have chemotherapy I
wasn't afraid

I am afraid of losing my hair   Dr Quigley split
the treatment to try and save my hair   my hair
is my biggest concern   she said there was no
guarantee   it's my appearance   I want to look
nice

my husband has been there with me every step
of the way   plus my parents

my mother literally walked in my footsteps   at
times when I was really weak, going through
chemotherapy and radiotherapy, she was there
and it must have been horrendous for her, but
she's been brilliant   six months before I was
diagnosed her younger sister died of ovarian
cancer and then to be told her only child had
breast cancer   she lost half a stone in a week

my father was very bitter but I said

Dad, I've got no answers for you, this is life, this
is fact   human beings get diseases

I tried to protect my dad a lot from the problems,
but he knew   the amount of times I'd come
out of treatment and find my dad sitting in the
waiting room and I'd say, Dad, don't worry
yourself, and he said

I needed to come and be here

14. Mary and Rebecca

MARY: one day she was convinced I was trying to take
her over   taking advantage of the illness to become her towering mother again   she rang up
and said

REBECCA: I want all my clothes

MARY: well, you've got them

REBECCA: I want all of them   you're keeping my clothes
from me

MARY: I was so furious   I had been washing and iron-
ing like a maniac   because she had a Hickman
line, sepsis was a problem, so I'd wash the
clothes and iron them all with a hot iron so we
couldn't in any way bring any infection in   so I
took all her clothes, including her see-through
blouses and her miniskirt, and her bikini, and I
gave them all to Joe, her father, and I was in
such a rage,

if she wants all her clothes she can have all
her clothes! if she wants them, bloody have
them   they're cluttering up my wardrobe! here
they are!

later, Rebecca said

REBECCA: when I saw the miniskirt I realised I'd gone too
          far, Mum

MARY: it's so hard to be real when the other person is
       so damned ill

15. Clare

CLARE: I am in this tiny space waiting for my turn there are five chairs lined up and a table, and on the table are some false flowers so it looks like a funeral parlour and I notice there is an ashtray with a cigarette stubbed out I was sitting there and this doctor came and sat down beside me

SIMON: I'm Simon, now can I call you Clare? do you want me to tell you the details?

CLARE: I thought that was wonderful he was treating me as a human being equal to him

everybody is sitting around the men are wearing little gowns but their bare legs are sticking out and they are wearing shoes and socks they are having pelvic radiotherapy like me some are quite old prostate? colon? there we all are, sitting there, and the men sit hunched up and looking worried with their heads in their hands, not looking important at all we all sat there and Simon said to me

SIMON: now you will probably have diarrhoea

CLARE: yes

SIMON: and we'll give you a sheet to tell you what you

can eat   you'll feel tired and you know you will
need dilators to put into your vagina   you'll
have to use them because not only will you
want your vagina to remain the same as it's always been but the doctors will want to examine
you so we need to make sure that your vagina
stays open

CLARE: I've never met him before

I sat there feeling absolutely shattered   falling
apart and trying not to show it   but I am in this
small space and all these people are near and
could hear everything   the women looked in-
terested and the men hid their faces in their
hands   I know the young doctor is doing his
best in an impossibly undignified situation

I long for privacy   I long for dignity

this, then, is radiotherapy

I lie down on this table   hard and narrow, and
there is this big solar system thing that comes
down   I keep my top on but I have to pull my
knickers and my tights down, and if I don't pull
them down far enough he will do it, he will pull
them down so they can see all my pubic parts
and it's so hard, very hard

[*she cries and then recovers*]

they gave me a little paper doily bit to keep my
modesty

16. Joan

JOAN: they put him upstairs in the hospice but I don't know it's the hospice   they couldn't really do anything more for Grant but the nurses were wonderful and they loved Grant

we used to play cards sometimes

then Grant's legs began swelling up and the skin was splitting, and Kim said

they're going to dress Grant's legs, you go out, Mum

but you see, I didn't do anything right   I came up with two milkshakes one day, I'd bought them in McDonald's   they loved milkshakes, the pair of them, and when I took them out of my bag there was none in there   I'd spilt it on the bus   I just wasn't with it   when I went into his room I said

well, I brought you two milkshakes, but look, my bag's wet and so is some bloke's arse

well, Grant had such a hearty laugh, and he laughed

don't make me laugh, it hurts

that's the only time I heard him say, it hurts

Grant started writing his own diary about how he felt   he hated it when he couldn't go to the toilet and it was all about that, really

well, I haven't been to the toilet again   they've given me some stuff and I still haven't gone

I said to him, do you get any pain? and he shouted

well, what do you think?

and I thought, oh dear, I'd better not say any more

Kim, I said, I don't think he wants me to come up the hospital, Kim, he's always digging at me   she said

he does, Mum, he loves you to come up

the nurse took me to see a counsellor   she said, when Grant dies   and I got up and I said, that's it, I'm not stopping in here, telling me my boy is going to die

Kim tried her hardest to tell me   she even got my best friend to tell me, and I said, don't talk to me like that, please, you can see how well he's eating   I wouldn't accept it

Kim ordered me lots of baskets and I started painting these baskets and I sewed ornamental flowers on them   sometimes, if I couldn't sleep over Grant, I'd get up in the middle of the night and work on my baskets one morning I went in and he was sitting on the bed, just sitting there on the edge   all alone   he said

my back is aching

so I go round and I sat the other side with my back against his to ease him, so we were back to back, me and Grant, and I could feel the heat of his body going right through me   we stayed like that for ages

Kim found her strength through sewing   her friend gave her this lovely material, she cut out these diamond shapes and all you saw Kim doing, even up the hospital, was sewing, sewing, sewing   she made the most beautiful quilt you've ever seen, that's what kept her going, and she never left his side   the baby, Sonny, went back to Antigua and Kim's husband, Winston, looked after her   she said to Winston

please look after Sonny, I'm not coming back till Grant goes

Kim even sleeps with Grant in the hospital now

17. Mary and Rebecca

MARY: Rebecca was desperate to get out of hospital for a while   she wanted to be somewhere else, to just be who she was   she wanted to escape   she didn't want to be ill any more

[*A* WOMAN *screams, off*]

REBECCA: shut up!

WOMAN: [*off*] I'm in pain!

REBECCA: everybody's in pain here and if you don't shut up I'll throttle you with my Hickman line

MARY: she was so passionate to get out, though she was very ill, that the doctor said she could if one of us would look after her, just for a night or two to give her a break from the hospital that she had begun to loathe

one morning she had to go back in to have her blood and chemo and she won't get up   I wake her and she goes back to sleep   I make some breakfast and call her again and she opens her eyes

REBECCA: I don't want it

MARY: and shuts them again

I'm not going to waste my time here, I'll pop back later, so I wrote her a card saying, ring when you're ready to go in because I've got stuff to do

so I leave this note on the bed beside her, which of course she sees, and as I get to the door she shouts

REBECCA: I'm coming! I'm coming! what's all the fuss about?

MARY: and I banged my head against the wall and I said

Rebecca, I can't do this   I don't know how to be with you

REBECCA: just be yourself

MARY: yeah, well, what is myself in these circumstances?

REBECCA: there's a wall between us

MARY: well, there's just going to have to be a wall between us   I can't do anything about that   I'll just have to be the chauffeur

it was so hard   it was real but it was horrible real   it wasn't how I wanted to be with her when she was that ill

18. Penny and Marilyn

PENNY: at six o'clock on Christmas Eve she collapses on the floor   the doorbell goes and it's our doctor

MARILYN: thank God you're here

PENNY: we get her into bed and he goes

she began to vomit black and diarrhoea at the same time   it got worse and worse and worse   the district nurse came round and then she went   and I am alone

and I went down into the garden and screamed into the night

on the third night, after having been sick for three days and three nights

MARILYN: ring the hospital

PENNY: I ring the hospital   keep her at home, see how she is tomorrow

I think she is going to die

MARILYN: ring the ambulance

PENNY: I ring the ambulance   we go to casualty   they give her a drip   Marilyn said

MARILYN: get your mum

PENNY: my mother came to the hospital   I was crying

Marilyn said to her

MARILYN: Penny has been wonderful   she has done everything for me

PENNY: my mother said, thank you for making Penny so happy

MARILYN: I stayed in hospital for a week then I came home again

a lovely community nurse came every day   he was called Neil and he was a mountaineer   the district nurse brought a water bed to make me more comfortable

PENNY: she is so thin   she is in pain

Marilyn wanted to die in a hospice

MARILYN: I don't want to die at home   I don't want to die in agony

PENNY: we went to the hospice   the doctor spent two hours with her

how do you feel?

MARILYN: it's wonderful to be here

PENNY: she was a very fastidious person   she liked clean things   the hospital wasn't clean enough

MARILYN: the hospice was spotless

PENNY: they looked after both of us

MARILYN: no more pain

PENNY: she still had style   she liked making the nurses laugh

on Sunday the doctor asked to speak to me

the cancer is everywhere   it's just a matter of time, he said

even then, she was still breathing, I still didn't think it was going to happen

she knew   she said

MARILYN: I've done everything, Pen, to look after you   you're going to be all right and I want you to live for both of us   I want you to make every day special

I don't mind if you meet someone half an hour after you bury me, I want you to be happy, Pen   enjoy life   you'll never be without me

PENNY: she couldn't protect me from her death   she wanted me to accept it   she said

MARILYN: thank you for everything

PENNY: she made me face it   she gave me strength

MARILYN: this is it, Pen, this is it   it's just you and me   no bullshit   everything is clear   this is it

PENNY: I love you   we were always meant to be together   always, always

I bring in pictures of her to show them how beautiful she was

MARILYN: I look so poorly now

PENNY: I want them to see what she really looks like

[*she holds up a photograph of* MARILYN]

MARILYN: I began to hallucinate   figures round the bed
Penny! I see people

PENNY: it's OK, darling, it's the morphine that's doing it,
there's no one else in the room

in a few days she was more or less unconscious
from the morphine

MARILYN: but she sleeps in a chair-bed by my side   Pen!
It's so dark

PENNY: they asked me if I'd like to see the chaplain   I
was so desperate I said yes   when he came he
was wearing a rainbow badge

MARILYN: they had got her a gay vicar!

19. Sharon

SHARON: I've always been a person who is very much my appearance and how I look to people   my hair used to be down there

> [*she points to below her waist*]

then one day I washed my hair and the bath was like that with hair

> [*she holds her hand high*]

and my mind just went   I thought, no, this isn't me, and I wrapped a towel round my head and I come downstairs and sit down near my husband and he said

what's up?

the bath is full of hair, and I started to cry

> [*she weeps*]

and Brian tried to think how he could deal with it   his way is action!

get ready, he said, we'll go up to Selfridge's and we'll buy you the best wig we can, I don't care how much money it costs

and that's what we did   NHS wigs you can tell and this was my fear   I don't like too much sympathy   I'd rather you said, you've done well, you've got through a lot

but from that time on I never lost my hair, it thinned but I never lost it and I never had to use the wig but it was a comfort knowing that it was there

20. Clare

CLARE: it is something to do with being recognised, it is recognition of who you are

when I went to Bart's I had an awful experience   I couldn't find the way   I couldn't find where I was meant to be

then they messed up my appointments   they didn't know who I was   they changed the times   one technician said to me, I don't know why they've put you in here

it's because I'm going to be away, I said

he hadn't bothered to look, and he was irritated because I wasn't following the exact times he wanted

the next time I came, he didn't have me on the list   I felt invisible   this huge giant thing takes over and the little you gets lost

why couldn't he say, yes, we've got you here, and we know who you are

it makes the biggest difference to be recognised, to be welcomed, to be told, yes, you are in the right place, yes, we are expecting you

21. Joan

JOAN: I went into his room and Grant is laying back and he is shaking and his eyes are looking straight ahead and I calls out, oh Kim, he's having a fit   and then he went still, and Kim said

Mum, he's gone, I felt him go

22. Mary and Rebecca

MARY: Rebecca was very keen on her sleep and if they wanted to give her blood in the night she made a huge song and dance and in the end, as it took two or three hours to go in, she made an arrangement with the sister that if the blood arrived after ten in the evening they would put it in the fridge and she could have it in the morning because she didn't want to be up all night   she had a Hickman line and she couldn't sleep because she worried about lying on it and the blood clotting

there was this really nice nurse who Rebecca knew well and she came in one night and said

BARBIE: I've got some blood for you, Rebecca

REBECCA: I don't have blood at this time   it's late, put it in the fridge

BARBIE: no, I want to give it to you now, Rebecca

REBECCA: no, I've made an arrangement with sister that I don't have blood after ten   talk to her

MARY: and this nurse put her hands on her hips and said jokingly

BARBIE: who's in charge here, Rebecca?

REBECCA: I am   I'm the patient   I have some choices over my life and I want to keep them

23. Penny and Marilyn

PENNY: at about three o'clock in the morning you came
            to and tried to talk   I can't make out

MARILYN: [*blurred speech*] I want you to me   postcards

PENNY: you wanted me to go home   the postcards

MARILYN: Vence

PENNY: you are desperately trying to find the right
            words

MARILYN: Vence

PENNY: I finally understand   you are talking about the
            visit to the chapel at Vence, and that an Italian
            family who had visited the hospice the day be-
            fore in tears

            please bring in a postcard to comfort them?

            the Matisse postcards?

MARILYN: yes, Matisse!

PENNY: I dashed home to fetch them

24. Clare

CLARE: one of the men I've gone on seeing on a daily basis he's one before me in radiotherapy and we say hello, but he's very huddled up and shy the other evening I was in a hurry, I had arranged to meet somebody for supper I was on time but they were running late so I said to the radiographer, I'm going to be late for an important appointment, and this man unhuddled himself and said

MAN: you can go before me

CLARE: thank you somebody else was having their treatment at the time so we talked

MAN: excuse me, could I ask you what you've got?

CLARE: I've got womb cancer and what have you got?

MAN: I've got bowel cancer I work for the Post Office I'm a night worker I go round in a van all night long I've gone back to work I wanted to be normal again my friends are all night workers when I was on the ward all my friends came to see me in the night we'd go into the waiting room and the nurses would bring us tea and coffee and sometimes even have a fag with us I've never been ill before and now I know everything about my bowels, everything about my insides

CLARE: yes, I know more about my insides now than I've ever known

MAN: I had a colostomy   as I was walking down the street I used to think everyone was looking at me and everyone knew I had cancer of the colon   I couldn't tell people at work at first   what was my boss going to say?   could I keep my job?

but the doctors have reversed it   I am so pleased   more pleased than I've ever been about anything

CLARE: and I told him about my Africa holiday

25. Sharon

SHARON: I don't want to be looked on as a victim   I
wanted to get back to how I was Sharon Sutton
before my diagnosis, and I've got there now   I
can put breast cancer in a compartment and
bring it out when I need to   and I get on with
my life   I don't wake up every morning thinking, my God, I've lost a breast   I pushed myself
to keep going   I needed to show myself that I
could do it, that I'm in charge   I needed to do
the most I could possibly do, so if there was a
spread of cells I had done everything I could

my parents are from the East End of London   my mother was one of seven children
and my grandfather died when he was forty-
two, leaving my nan with a very young family
and in those days it was very hard and I think
my nan and my mum both got strength from
that   as a child she's gone without shoes, she's
gone without food   once my nan pawned the
hearth that went round the fire just to get
food   and when you've come from nothing,
and that type of upbringing, she had to be
strong

Dr Quigley laughs every time I go to see
her   I've always got questions to ask and she's

really good, she will always answer them   I
walk in and I said, what's all this about anti-
perspirants and breast cancer?   I saw it on
the internet   no, no, she said, nothing is
proved   she has always been able to answer my
questions

she does a very hard job   she faces people who
are very afraid and in despair and she can't say
to them as a doctor, don't worry, I can cure you,
take this tablet, go away

to deal with that day in day out

26. Mary and Rebecca

MARY: what I've learnt is you can't just make good stuff happen   all you can do is just live with it being horrible   if there's a wall between us it's heartbreaking but so be it   I couldn't make it nice   but much later she said

REBECCA: I don't want anyone   I can't bear anyone around   I don't want anyone near me

MARY: hang on, I'll go, then

REBECCA: no, no, you're different   I don't mean you at all   I can't take anybody else

you've got to be here

MARY: we'd broken through that boundary   in the sense that I was somewhere in the right place with her   somehow   most of the time   we'd bloody well earned it even so

it seemed very unique to me   it was my struggle   it was a struggle   then I began to worry   had I made her too dependent on me?   she had a boyfriend in Sint Maarten but he wasn't able to come too much and because I was working freelance I was the only person who could be there   her father lived in Wales   I could just stop working   there was a temptation to want to be the most important person, which I had to resist or I would be exploiting her I had to just somehow keep it real I wanted to be a saint, there was no doubt about it, but Rebecca challenged this she got enraged with me

REBECCA: get off!

[MARY *laughs*]

MARY: I'd think I've got it, at last I've got it, I've got the hang of it now, thank you

then the next day something different would be needed so I could never rest on my learning, there was always something new to be struggled with it's so rough, so diabolical, that combination of sadness for the person, compassion for the person, enragement at all the stuff that's been taken away from you the life and the richness you're getting, it brings up a lot of shadow things, you're in the shadow the whole time, living it, digging round in it

27. Clare

CLARE: I want to be told you're not forgotten   someone
at work sent me the minutes, saying, I know
you're not at work but you might like to have a
look at what's happening   she includes me and
recognises me as someone who is coming back
to work

I am not a forgotten person

28. Mary and Rebecca

REBECCA: I want to have as much fun as I can

MARY: but I wanted her to stay alive and not risk anything and when she had visitors I wanted to say,
isn't it time they all went?   you're looking very
tired, darling   I had to bite that one back but I
could really feel it welling up   I was itching to
get rid of them all

[REBECCA *is laughing*]

MARY: if Rebecca was having a wonderful time with
her cousin I didn't need to get rid of the cousin
so I could be good to her   I had to step back and
not take control of her life   Rebecca wanted to
be treated like a living person and not like a dying person

[REBECCA *is still laughing*]

REBECCA: I'm alive now, not dying, living

29. Joan

JOAN: I don't know what happened then but I ended up in another room and the nurse gave me a drink and then Kim came in

come on, Mum, you've got to say goodbye to Grant

so I go back into the room with her and I cuddle him up, and then I don't want to let go of him because he is still lovely and warm   I was cuddling round his neck

later we sit in the room, me and Kim, and Grant is just laying in the bed   he is peaceful   the whole of the swelling had gone

when we got back to the flat I took off my clothes and got straight into Grant's bed   it was a hospital bed they had lent us   I could feel Grant there   he was here in this flat   so strange

30. Penny and Marilyn

PENNY: when she died there was a rainbow in the room

there was no rush at the hospice   I stayed with her a long time   I lay down on the bed next to her   I felt her love   then my mum came and fetched me

they came and took her corneas   that's what she wanted   I had a handwritten letter from Moorfields saying they had gone to two people   that meant a lot

before I met Marilyn I had a lot of love affairs

MARILYN: but after she met me she only wanted me

she went to Fortnum and Mason and bought the wine for the funeral

PENNY: she was a very stylish woman, was Marilyn

31. Clare

CLARE:　I went for my follow-up　I had this West Indian registrar　he was just the best-looking man you ever saw in your life, wonderful looking　he was tall and willowy and he had this wonderful face, wonderful　big black, dark eyes and a very kind wonderful face　he said

WEST INDIAN DOCTOR: you've got to be careful with me because I don't understand the idiom　I'm new to the country and when you say something I might not understand it

CLARE:　I felt he was giving me power by saying this　he was telling me, he hadn't got everything taped

WEST INDIAN DOCTOR: is there anything worrying you?

CLARE:　he examined me and felt my glands

WEST INDIAN DOCTOR: your glands are a little up, have you had a cold?

CLARE:　yes

WEST INDIAN DOCTOR: then I am not in the least bit worried

CLARE:　but I have stiff neck　it is sometimes really painful, I'm very frightened that it's cancer

WEST INDIAN DOCTOR: I'm absolutely sure that it's not, but medicine is so strange that I can't tell you for sure that it's not

CLARE: and he sent me for an x-ray of my neck   he took care of me

32. Sharon

SHARON: I've cut out red meat   little things to try and
          help myself so cancer doesn't rule me, I rule it   I
          know all the long words, I can understand and
          ask what I need to know

          sometimes I have to face the results of different
          tests and the tests could mean my cancer has
          come back, and that is horrible, to wait in a
          waiting room and to know you are going to
          hear if your cancer can be treated or it's spread
          too far and it's just a case of how long they can
          keep you alive, and to be able to get up and walk
          into that room, the incredible strength involved,
          I don't know where it comes from

          and then I go for the liver scan, my parents are
          with me, and the fellow does the scan   he is
          very sweet, he knows how frightened I am

          he said to me, your heart is beating so fast and I
          said to him, if you thought you had a tumour on
          your liver your heart would be beating fast

          he was only a young fellow and he smiles and
          after I'd had the test and the tape was due to go
          back to Dr Quigley, he looked at me and he said,
          very quietly

don't worry, no problem there

and that was so nice of him because I had to go
home and I had to wait two days to see the doctor and I would have been thinking about it all
those two days

33. Mary and Rebecca

MARY: Rebecca told her boyfriend in Sint Maarten, on the phone, that she may not be going to make it

REBECCA: I may not be going to make it

MARY: then she told me that's what she had said to him

REBECCA: I may not be going to make it

MARY: I said to her doctor

is she dying?

because if she is we should be getting her to a hospice or getting her better nursing or something   you only put up with this if you're going to come through

we haven't given up on her, he said

as if I had

34. Clare

CLARE: I don't want to be told I shouldn't feel anxious and depressed because that's what I am feeling   it comes and goes   it's very fluid   I want to be left with that   I don't want that to be taken away from me because it's real

35. Joan

JOAN: it took nine months from the day they told us he had cancer till the day he died

after he died and we read his little book it said, my mum can't cope with this cancer   she does everything wrong and it makes me laugh

36. Sharon

SHARON: I don't ask why me?   because why anybody?   when you're ill you want something to
blame but there's nothing to blame   this is just
something that's happened to me, there is no
answer to the reason why   it's just a case of
carrying on   I get up in the morning and I live
for this day   nobody can plan too far ahead,
you never know what's going to happen   what
comes, comes   and other people can't give you
the strength, you have to find the strength in
yourself

as for me right now

I'm well   I'm clear

I'm lucky

37. Mary and Rebecca

MARY: the nurses were very busy and she was having a lot of medication that wasn't very nice   by then she let us be there all the time   she needed us there   I wanted to be sure it was worth it, that what she was going through had some purpose

she had a lot of complications because of the steroids   she had a lot of pain in her stomach

in the end they got in an abdominal surgeon to see if she could be operated on   he came and said to us

SURGEON: I've got two consultants I work to and one of them has said I recommend operating and the other one has said I should leave her alone so I've decided I'm going to make my own judgements on this

I want to see her alone   this is between me and Rebecca

MARY: then he went in and saw her

when he came out, we are sitting outside on this little bench, her father and me, and he crouched down beside us and said

SURGEON: this is really difficult because you don't know me and I don't know you but what I have to say is this young lady is dying and she should be left in peace and that's my recommendation

MARY: and it was wonderful because it was so straight   he told us her immune system was in collapse   she's in a lot of distress   she should be made comfortable

then he went and talked to James and Sara, her brother and sister, who were sitting a little way away, and sat down

SURGEON: I've just seen your sister and if she were my sister I would say she should be let be and made comfortable because I think she's going to die

MARY: he was so straight   he was wonderful   he was clear   then you know what to do   you have the truth and you've got to deal with it   you've got some certainty, you're not having to guess all the time

and that's the kind of connection, using expertise and professionalism in a really human way, not making a big deal of it   it's not having to be a good listener or having to understand about death, it's just dealing with it in a very pragmatic and sensitive, not soppy, way, but just knowing what was going on

that's what seemed so hard for the consultants to do, they just didn't know if they were coming or going in that   they could have added a lot by telling us clearly what was going on   to have said sooner, she is dying, then we could begin to get our heads round it

it wouldn't matter perhaps so much if you weren't going to die, but there is something about the dying of it that's so important   the transition between being a person who is going to make it to one who is going to die   they don't have a way of being in that transitional moment

specially tough for the parents of grown-up children   you have a role but can't really make any important decisions   it is very confusing   how to be and where to be

38. Clare

CLARE: what makes you into a good doctor is being
humble, being able to learn from people

but I think it must be agonising to work with
people that are going to die   that gives you the
edge, the importance, being in a position where
you are expected to cure and you can't and
you're battling with death and often not winning

for me, I feel thankful   I feel grateful

I'm still alive

39. Mary and Rebecca

MARY: and a few days later Rebecca had this palliative cocktail to help her with her pain and she did a complete collapse into unconsciousness and the sister said we could just let her go because she's going to go anyway

and I said, no, I think she's entitled to some lucidity, she shouldn't just go off by mistake

can you turn around what you've just given her?

they had an antidote and they gave it to her   it seemed terribly important to me that she should know what was happening to her when it was happening

she speaks, but didn't make too much sense and I leave the room so the doctor can examine her and he comes out and says to me, Mrs Sitwell, Rebecca would like to talk to you now

and I went in and she looked at me and completely lucidly she said

REBECCA: Mum, it's time to let go

MARY: all right, sweetheart

and I went out and told the doctor I'd said to Rebecca I'd back her up if this moment came it must have been the toughest moment of my whole life

I went back in and I said

OK, Rebecca

and she pulled off the oxygen mask   typically impatient and irascible   let's get on with it

and they kept on the pain relief and the things that made her comfortable and stopped everything else

this nurse put all her other patients off onto other nurses and she came and sat with us while we sat with Rebecca and she said

I don't want to be invasive and I won't stay if you don't want me to

but it was brilliant having her there because she knew about death and we didn't   we didn't know how to help her or what to do and when Rebecca got restless and we went to soothe her, she said

it's all right, just let her be, you don't need to fuss, just let her go in her own time

and she just sat there for two or three hours just to be with us while we were with Rebecca, which made such a huge difference

and then she sent James and Sara off to get a cup of tea   this nice nurse, she was so there, and so aware of what was happening   it was so helpful for us to have some guidance in how to be in those last hours   and after a while she said

I think you should get them back again

she watched her breathing, she said

I don't think she's conscious any more but she may be able to hear what you say

when Rebecca died, Sara and James were there and her father was there   we were all there with her when she died

a young woman who was in the ward with Rebecca said her best memory of her was when they were waiting together for their chemo, which was late

Rebecca shouted down the corridor

REBECCA: who do you have to fuck around here to get your chemo on time?

MARY: when she told me that, it was as if Rebecca blew through the room

THE END

By the same author

STEAMING

Steaming is set in the Turkish Room of a run-down Public Baths in the East End of London, where five women regularly meet, to bathe, relax, and share their troubles.

Originally produced at the Theatre Royal, Stratford East, with Georgina Hale, Maria Charles and Brenda Blethyn

'a lovely play, suffused with affection' – Ned Chaillet, *The Times*

'[a] funny and touching play' – Douglas Orgill, *Daily Express*

'full of lively, ribald humour' – Christopher Hudson, *New Standard*

For a free copy of our complete list of plays and theatre books write to:
Amber Lane Press, Church Street,
Charlbury, Oxon OX7 3PR, UK
Telephone and fax: 01608 810024
E-mail: info@amberlane press.co.uk